Festivals of the World

KENYA

Gareth Stevens Publishing
MILWAUKEE

Written by
FALAQ KAGDA

Edited by
ELIZABETH BERG

Designed by
HASNAH MOHD ESA

First published in North America in 1997 by
Gareth Stevens Publishing
1555 North RiverCenter Drive, Suite 201
Milwaukee, Wisconsin 53212 USA

For a free color catalog describing Gareth Stevens' list of high-quality books and multimedia programs, call
1-800-542-2595 (USA)
or 1-800-461-9120 (Canada).
Gareth Stevens Publishing's Fax: (414) 225-0377.
See our catalog, too, on the World Wide Web:
http://gsinc.com

Printed in Singapore

Originated and designed by
Times Books International
an imprint of Times Editions Pte Ltd
Times Centre, 1 New Industrial Road
Singapore 536196

Library of Congress Cataloging-in-Publication Data
Kagda, Falaq.
Kenya / by Falaq Kagda.
p. cm. — (Festivals of the world)
Includes bibliographical references and index.
Summary: Describes how the culture of Kenya is reflected in its many festivals, including Jamburi, Eunoto, and Kenyatta Day.
ISBN 0-8368-1685-4 (lib. bdg.)
1. Festivals—Kenya—Juvenile literature.
2. Kenya—Social life and customs—Juvenile literature. [1. Festivals—Kenya. 2. Kenya—Social life and customs.] I. Title. II. Series.
GT4889.K4K34 1997
394.2'696762—dc20 96-32491

2 3 4 5 6 7 8 9 99 98

CONTENTS

It's Festival Time . . .

There are many different kinds of people of Kenya and many different beliefs, so you have your choice of festivals. Do you want to go traditional? Join us for Initiation and Eunoto. Or come celebrate Palm Sunday with the Christians, or the Prophet's birthday with the Muslims. But, anyway, be sure to join us for Kenya's birthday. You can hear the drumming now, and the warriors are marching in with their ostrich feather headdresses. Come on, it's festival time in Kenya . . .

Where's Kenya?

Kenya is located on the eastern coast of Africa, south of Ethiopia, west of Somalia, and north of Tanzania. The country gets its name from Mount Kenya, an extinct volcano (it hasn't erupted in hundreds of years) that was once higher than Mount Everest. Kenya is a peaceful and successful country. Its capital, Nairobi, is one of the largest and most modern cities in Africa. Kenya is also known for its wild animal reserves. Only a few miles from Nairobi's tall skyscrapers, cheetahs and elephants run free.

Who are the Kenyans?

Kenya is home to a wide variety of people. There are Europeans and Indians who came when Kenya was a colony of Great Britain. There are descendents of the Arab traders who settled on the coast. But mostly there are people from over 40 African tribes who came to this area at different times and stayed. Africans belong to four main groups: Khoisan, Cushites, Nilotes, and Bantus. Of these, only the Khoisan no longer live in Kenya. The largest tribe is the Kikuyu. Other large tribes are the Kamba, the Luo, and the Luaya. The Maasai are well known for their colorful dress. They are one of the last tribes to give up their traditional lifestyle.

A little Maasai girl with a friendly smile. Girls and women of the Maasai tribe shave their heads.

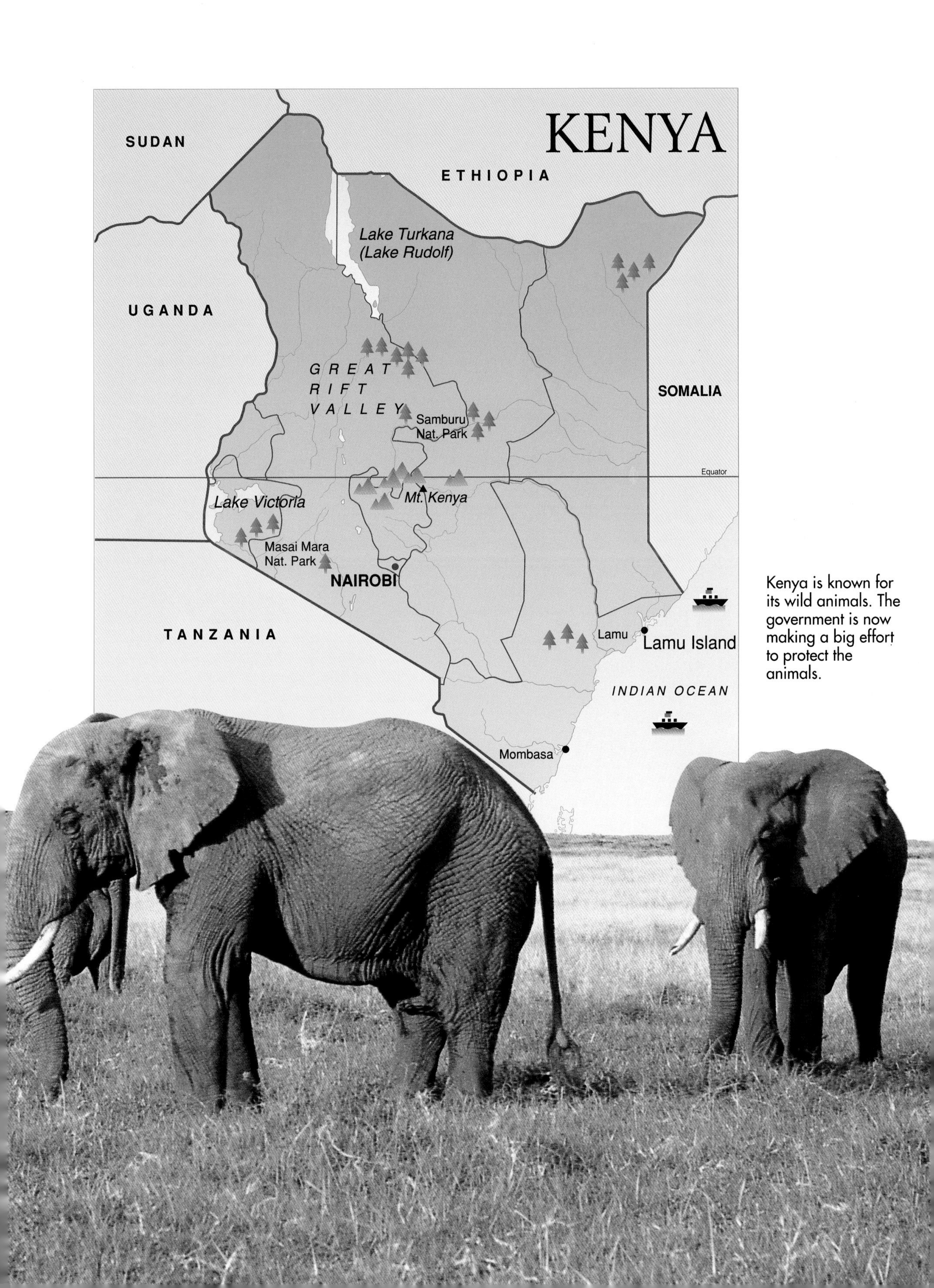

Kenya is known for its wild animals. The government is now making a big effort to protect the animals.

When's the Celebration?

When a Kenyan celebrates festivals depends on what his or her religion is. Christians follow the same calendar as you probably do, and celebrate the same festivals as Christians in the rest of the world. Muslims follow a **lunar** calendar, and their holidays move back 11 days each year. In traditional African societies, the most important festivals don't happen at a particular time of year. Instead, they celebrate the passage from one period of life to another.

SPRING

- **SAFARI RALLY**—Sports cars race all around Kenya. At first, Europeans always won, but now the winner is almost always Kenyan.
- **EASTER**

Come on and dance with me at Jamburi on page 11.

SUMMER

- **MADARAKA DAY**—Celebrates the anniversary of self-government.
- **MOMBASA AGRICULTURAL SHOW**

AUTUMN

- **KENYATTA DAY**—Marks the anniversary of Jomo Kenyatta's arrest by the British in 1952.
- **MALINDI FISHING FESTIVAL**

WINTER

- **JAMBURI** (Independence Day)
- **CHRISTMAS**

TRADITIONAL AFRICAN CELEBRATIONS

- **PIERCING OF EARS**—Children have the outer edge of their ears pierced when they are 4 or 5 years old, then the lobes are pierced at around 10 years.
- **INITIATION** ✪ **EUNOTO** ✪ **MARRIAGE**
- **BIRTH OF FIRST CHILD**—Parents achieve a higher status after their first child is born.
- **ELDER**—Before the oldest child is circumcised, parents go through a two-day cleansing ceremony to become elders.
- **SENIOR ELDER**—Senior elders carry a staff made of a sacred tree and a bunch of leaves. They can now administer justice.
- **DIGNIFIED ELDER**—Dignified elders wear special brass earrings. They decide the dates of circumcisions.

MUSLIM FESTIVALS

- **ID AL-FITRI**—Marks the end of the fasting month of Ramadan. Muslims celebrate with feasting and prayers in the mosque.
- **ID AL-ADHA**—Marks Abraham's willingness to sacrifice his son, Isaac.
- **MAULIDI AL NEBI**

The best dancing is happening at Maulidi. Join us on page 25.

JAMBURI

The sound of tribal drumming fills the air. Tall warriors come marching down the street, wearing ostrich feather headdresses and carrying spears and brightly decorated shields. You can hear shouts of "Uhuru!" [oo-HOO-roo] (that means "Freedom" in **Swahili**, the language people speak on the East African coast). Row after row of colorful tribes march by in their traditional clothing. This is the parade for Jamburi, Kenyan Independence Day, in Nairobi. It is a day for all Kenyans to come together and celebrate their country. "**Harambee**!" [ha-ram-BAY] they shout, "Let us work together!"

Left: A drummer from the Chuka tribe in traditional dress.

Opposite: Jomo Kenyatta is sworn in as the first prime minister of the new country of Kenya on December 13, 1964. Kenyatta was never without his fly whisk, a traditional emblem of power in many African tribes. You can make your own fly whisk—look on page 28.

Harambee!

Harambee was the favorite word of Kenya's first president, Jomo Kenyatta. Kenyatta worked for many years to free Kenya from British rule. After independence came on December 13, 1964, he led the new country until his death. Kenya is a country of many peoples—40 different ethnic groups live there, and they speak many different languages. For the new country to survive, Kenyatta knew everyone would have to work together. He told people that the government didn't have much money to help them build the things they needed, like schools or community centers. When there were things they needed, they would have to work together to build them. People organized Harambee fundraisers, where everyone helps out to make something the community needs.

Kikuyu people put on a Jamburi parade in a small town.

Choosing an anthem

One day not long before Kenya became an independent country, Jomo Kenyatta and his advisors were listening to music. They were trying to choose music for the national anthem, but they couldn't decide. Then Kenyatta noticed that children had gathered outside to listen. "Why not let them choose?" he said. So they played the music for the children. All the children agreed on one song: an African lullaby sung by mothers to their children. The national anthem of Kenya is called "Es Mungu Nguvu Yetu" ("O God of All Creation"). It's a very beautiful anthem.

Above: A corps of women soldiers marches in the Independence Day parade in Nairobi.

Schoolchildren singing at Jamburi celebrations.

A lot of changes

Building their country has not been easy for Kenyans. Not long ago, almost all Kenyans lived in the countryside. Now many of these people have moved to Nairobi or some other large city. Their lives have changed greatly. They no longer wear traditional dress. They wear clothes much like yours. They work in factories and offices instead of out in the countryside herding cows. They live in apartments instead of round mud houses. They speak English or Swahili instead of their native language. And they live among a variety of people instead of only their fellow tribespeople. What a change! But even if they miss the old ways, life is slowly getting better for Kenyans.

Think about this

Jomo Kenyatta was well loved by his people. Kenyans fondly referred to him as ***Mzee*** [em-ZAY], which means "Old One" or "Wise One" in Swahili. Through his leadership, Kenya became a peaceful and prosperous country.

Dancing is an important part of African celebrations. In traditional cultures, dancing is often reserved for certain special occasions.

INITIATION

A group of boys stand in a circle, singing songs of encouragement to the ones who in the morning will face the greatest moment in their lives. Some of the songs are taunting. They say that the boys are cowards and will run away. The others sing back in reply that they are brave and will face the knife with courage. After this round of singing, the boys leave the ***boma*** [BOH-ma] (that's the village where they live). In the morning, they will come running in to where everyone waits. They will throw off their ***chuka*** [CHOO-kah], the cloak that Maasai men and boys wear, and lie on a special goatskin. The circumciser, his face painted with white chalk, will raise the knife and begin his work.

A test of courage

This is the Maasai **circumcision** ceremony. Every Maasai boy must pass this test of courage when he is around 15 years old. How he acts during these few minutes will bring either honor or disgrace to his family and his people. If he shows any sign of emotion, he will be branded a coward. At the end of this ceremony, he will no longer be a child. He will be a man. If the elders decide that he is especially brave, honest, and a good speaker, he may even become ***olaiguenani***. The olaguenani leads the others of his age throughout life. It is a great honor to be named olaiguenani.

Boys waiting to be circumcised.

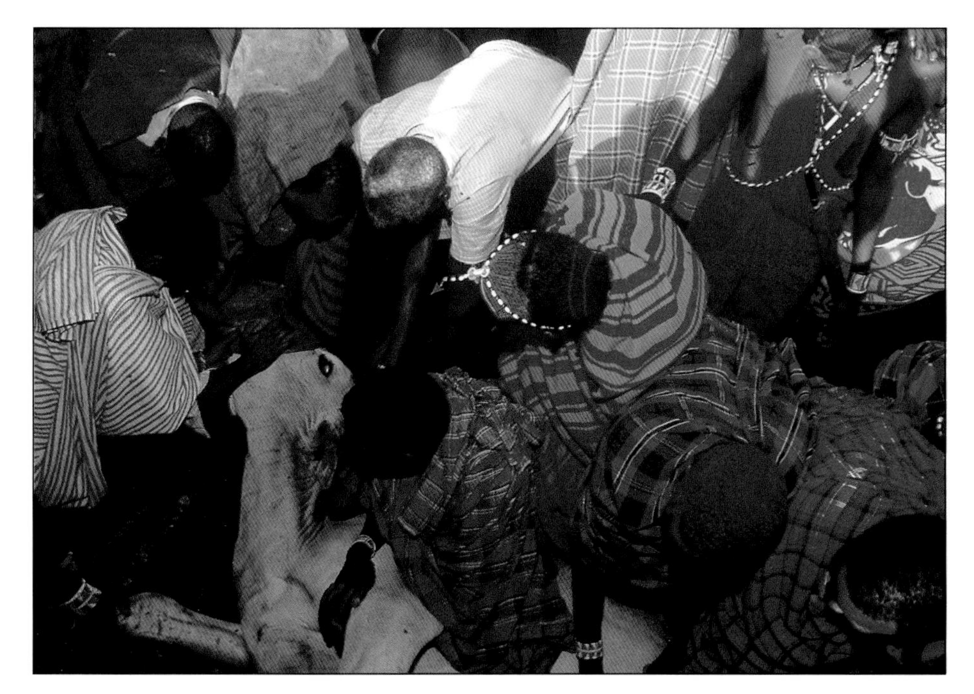

Everyone gathers around for the sacrifice.

Time to eat

After the circumcisions are finished, it is time to celebrate. While each boy goes to his mother's hut to rest, a bull is sacrificed and roasted, and everyone sits down to eat. The Maasai are traditionally cattle herders. They are very fond of cows. A Maasai judges how rich a man is by how many cows he owns, so they rarely kill cows. Instead they drink milk and blood from the cow. They would only kill one of their animals for an important ceremony like a circumcision.

After the ceremony, a young olive tree is planted for each boy. This symbolizes his new life as an adult member of the community. He has entered a new stage of life, and with it comes a new set of responsibilities.

An elder chews on a piece of meat. Maasai eat meat only at very special festivals.

What are age sets?

Instead of celebrating the seasons or the farming cycle or religious holidays, like people do in many other parts of the world, the Maasai celebrate the different stages of life. Like most traditional peoples of Kenya, the Maasai group people together in **age sets**. All the boys and girls who were circumcised at the same time are part of one age set. The members of an age set remain very close throughout their lives. Together they go through all the rituals that mark the different stages of life. Each age set is given a name that refers to some important event that happened at that time.

During the period that follows the ceremony, the boys shoot birds and stuff them to make a headdress. Newly circumcised boys wear black chukas instead of the usual red one.

Learning to hunt and handle a spear is an important part of moran life.

Think about this
The Maasai keep track of their history through the age sets. Each age set is given a name that refers to something that happened about the time they were circumcised. Later, people remember their history by refering to the age sets.

The next stage

After being circumcised, boys become ***moran***. Moran were once the warriors of the tribe. They protected the others from other tribes and from wild animals, such as the lions who roam around Maasailand. Now the moran mostly hunt lions and steal cattle to prove their bravery. The Maasai believe that all cattle were given to them by their god, **Ngai** [EN-guy]. When they take other people's cattle, they believe they are only reclaiming what is theirs. The moran live together in bush camps. It is a fun time for them.

Warriors and students

The Maasai have held on to their traditions longer than most Kenyans. When the Europeans first came to East Africa, the Maasai were fierce warriors who terrorized all the neighboring tribes. Today, their traditions are slowly disappearing. Instead of becoming warriors, many young Maasai men choose to stay in school. They hope that if they get an education they will have a better life.

Members of an age set become very close. These young moran will probably remain close throughout their lives as they go through all the big events in their lives together.

THE GIRLS' TURN

Women are the head of the house in traditional African society. That's because they build the houses themselves! The husband is not even allowed to enter the house without his wife's permission. The work of men and women, and the rituals they go through, are very different. Girls also go through initiation, and they are also circumcised at this time, but the ceremony is often quite different. In many tribes, like the Maasai, the girls' circumcision is done privately with little ceremony. In other tribes, like the Kikuyu, girls participate in initiation ceremonies just like the boys.

Kikuyu girls with faces painted for circumcision.

A Kikuyu initiation

Two days before, the parents of the young people to be circumcised have a big feast. They sit in a circle. One by one, the young people are called in to be blessed. A senior elder marks symbols on their faces with a white chalk that comes from Mount Kenya, where the Kikuyu believe Ngai resides. An old woman from the ceremonial council then anoints each child with oil. The rest of the elders give their blessings. Then the girls return home, where they are met by the young women of their **clan**, who sing, dance, and jump with joy.

A Maasai girl wears black after circumcision.

Kikuyu initiation ceremonies include a full day of dancing and singing.

The great dance

The day before the circumcision, the girl has her head shaved and is clothed in beads loaned to her by women relatives and friends. A rattle is put around her right knee. Then, led by her relatives and friends dressed in their best clothes, she marches in procession to the house where the ceremony will take place. There all the young people who are to be circumcised dance and sing all day. The next day they are circumcised.

A long vacation

For three or four months after circumcision, the new initiates do no work. They spend their days singing special songs. At the end of this time, there is a big festival where they are introduced to the community as new adult members. While the initiates dance, their parents feast and drink beer.

EUNOTO

It's the night of the full moon in Maasailand. The boys who were circumcised in the last group have now been moran for about 12 years. They are ready to go on to the next stage in their lives. As the kudu horn sounds, the warriors enter in a long procession. They march in single file in groups of 20 to 30 at a time. You can hear the clanging of the bells tied around their thighs. As they walk, they chant. For the last time, they wear their lion headdresses and carry their shields. They wear red cloths around their hips, and their hair is long and stained red. This is their last chance to enjoy the moran life. For four days they will sing and dance and participate in the rituals that conclude their time as moran.

What happens at Eunoto?

Eunoto is a very important ceremony. The festivities go on for four or five days. A special village is constructed just for Eunoto. Everyone stays in this ceremonial village during the festival, except the graduating moran, who go back to their bush camps at night. Two bulls are sacrificed to feed all the people.

A moran wearing a very fancy ostrich feather headdress.

The only time you can hear the kudu horn is at Eunoto. The kudu horn announces the arrival of the moran.

A pilgrimage up the mountain

On the third day, everyone makes a pilgrimage up Mount Suswa to a sacred tree. There they sacrifice an ox. The warriors paint their faces with white chalk. The elders of the community give the new senior warriors a new group name and bless them. The elders also choose an ***olotuno*** for the group. The olotuno is the leader of this group. He then selects a bride to show that the graduating moran may now marry. At the end of the ceremony, the warriors run down the mountain back to the camp.

A group of moran come down from their bush camp to participate in Eunoto.

Rows of shields lined up. Eunoto is a time to put away shields and headdresses.

Think about this
Because life in Kenya has changed so much since Independence, many of the old traditions are dying out. The last Eunoto was celebrated in 1985. There will probably not be another one.

It's graduation time

Eunoto marks the young men's graduation from their time as junior warriors to the status of senior warriors. They will no longer go out hunting lions and stealing cattle. They will no longer wear their warrior trappings. They will no longer live together in camps. They must settle down now and become the responsible adults of the community. After Eunoto, they have the right to get married and to own property. Traditionally, they go into cattle trading. Today, many go back to school or look for a job. Eunoto is their last chance to act wild. For many, it is a sad time, because their days of freedom and adventure are ending.

Right: This is the moran dance, in which they jump straight up. Some moran are able to jump very high.

Opposite: The high point of the ceremonies is when the graduating moran's mother shaves his head. This is the most solemn moment of a man's life, for it marks the end of his youth. Some moran tremble or faint when their head is shaved.

Christians and Muslims

Many people in Kenya follow traditional African religions, but there are also many who have converted to Christianity, and Islam has been the main religion on the coast for many centuries. Also, a lot of Kenyans combine traditional practices with Christianity. There are many different Christian sects in Kenya.

Communion at a village in Kenya.

How do Christians celebrate?

Kenyan Christians celebrate their holidays in much the same way as Christians in the United States, but in some ways they have made the celebrations more African. There is a lot of singing and dancing in Kenyan churches. Festivals are a big social event, with festivities going on at the church all day long. Palm Sunday is an important holiday celebrated with processions to the church.

Left: A Kenyan Roman Catholic priest.

Opposite: A Palm Sunday procession marches to the Catholic church.

Come to Maulidi

Through most of the year, Lamu is a quiet little island where donkey carts and boats are the only transportation, but shortly after Easter, Lamu fills with thousands of people. They come from East and North Africa, Saudi Arabia, and the Arabian Gulf to pray at the open-air worships under the stars and join in the singing and dancing in the square in front of Riyadha Mosque.

What are they celebrating?

This is the Maulidi al Nebi, the birthday of the Prophet. It is an important holiday for Muslims because it is when Muslims honor Muhammad. Muslims believe that Muhammad was the last in a line of prophets that includes Moses and Jesus Christ. The Koran, the Muslim holy book, was written down by the Prophet. Maulidi is a time for Muslims to think about Muhammad and his teachings.

A little girl reads the Koran. At Maulidi, Muslims pray and study the Koran.

Muslim drummers playing at Maulidi.

Think about this
Both Christianity and Islam have had to adapt to traditional African practices. Christianity is a recent arrival in Kenya, and people are still trying to adapt this new religion to fit better with African ways.

Who are the Muslims in Kenya?

There are many Muslims living along the coast of East Africa. Many centuries ago, Arab traders sailed down the eastern coast of Africa in search of new places to trade. They started settlements all along the coast. As the years went by, the Arabs mixed with the **Bantu** peoples of the area. The local people converted to Islam. They started using many Arabic words in their language. This mixture of Arabic and Bantu (a native African language) is called Swahili. It is spoken all over the coast of East Africa. The Swahili people wear clothes that look much like those worn by Arabs in the Middle East. They also follow customs that are a mixture of African and Arab traditions.

The ritual sword fight is one of the high points of the Maulidi celebration in Lamu.

Things For You To Do

Wherever you go in Africa, you will see people sitting over a game board or even a group of holes in the ground, moving pebbles from one cup to another. This game goes by many different names. In Kenya, it is called Kigogo [kih-GO-go]. Would you like to try playing it? To make a quick Kigogo board, take an egg carton and cut off the top. Each player takes one side. You also need a store for captured pieces and 48 marbles, seeds, or beans. And you need two people to play.

How to play Kigogo

To start, put four marbles, seeds, or beans in each cup. The first player picks up all the marbles from any cup on his or her side of the board. Starting with the next cup to the right, put one marble in each cup. When you drop the last marble into a cup that doesn't have three or no marbles in it already, pick up all of the marbles in that cup. Then start again with the next cup on the right and put one marble in each cup. If there are three marbles in the last cup, pick up all four marbles and put them in your store. Then it's the other person's turn. If there are no marbles in the last cup, it's the end of your turn. During the first player's turn, the other player collects marbles for his or her bank every time the first player drops a fourth marble into a cup that already has three, unless that was the first player's last marble.

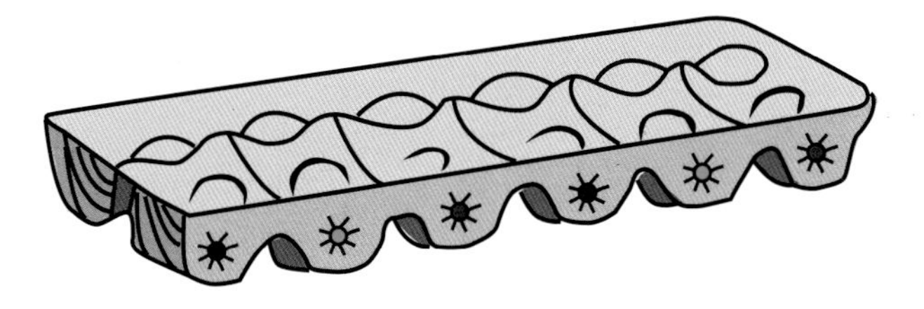

Who wins?

The game continues until all the marbles are collected in the players' stores. The player who collects the next-to-last four marbles gets the last four as a bonus. Whoever collects the most marbles wins that round and takes over a cup on the other player's side. Go on playing until one player has taken all of the other's cups.

Things to look for in your library

A Great Day Out: African Life, African Words. Ken and Audra Wilson-Max. (Chronicle Books, 1996).
African Rhythms: Songs from Kenya. D. Nzomo (Asch Records).
Beneath the Rainbow: A Collection of Chidren's Stories and Poems from Kenya. Sam Mbure, Valerie Cuthbert, and Kariuki Gakuo (Jacaranda Designs, 1995).
Dropping in on Kenya. David C. King (Rourke Publishing Group, 1995).
How the Ostrich Got its Long Neck: A Tale from the Akamba of Kenya. Verna Aardema (Scholastic, 1995).
Jomo Kenyatta: President of Kenya. Dennis Wepman, ed. (Chelsea House, 1985).
Kenya. Karen Jacobsen (Children's Press, 1991).
The Kitchen Toto (Cannon Films, 1988).
The Maasai. Tujambe Zeleza (Rosen Publishing Group, 1994).
Postcards from Kenya. Helen Arnold (Raintree/Steck Vaughn, 1991).

Make a Fly Whisk

Important people in Kenya traditionally carry a fly whisk as a mark of their rank. Fly whisks are made from animal tails. A very special one might be made from an elephant tail with a gold-plated handle. A cow or horse tail with a leather handle is more common, and a child might use a goat tail. Here's an idea for an imitation fly whisk.

You will need:

1. A ball of raffia (or you could use yarn or twine)
2. A piece of cardboard 5" x 4" (12 x 10 cm)
3. A piece of fringe
4. Aluminium foil
5. Colored tape
6. Scissors
7. An Xacto knife
8. 12" (30 cm) braid or cord
9. A pencil
10. A ruler

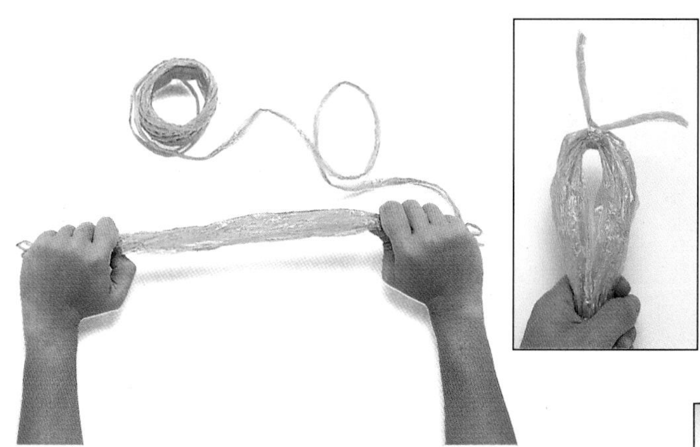

1 Cut the raffia in 40″ (1 m) lengths until you have enough for a nice, full tail. Tie all the pieces together in the middle.

2 Tear the raffia lengthwise so that it gets bushy (or fray the yarn or string by pulling the strands apart).

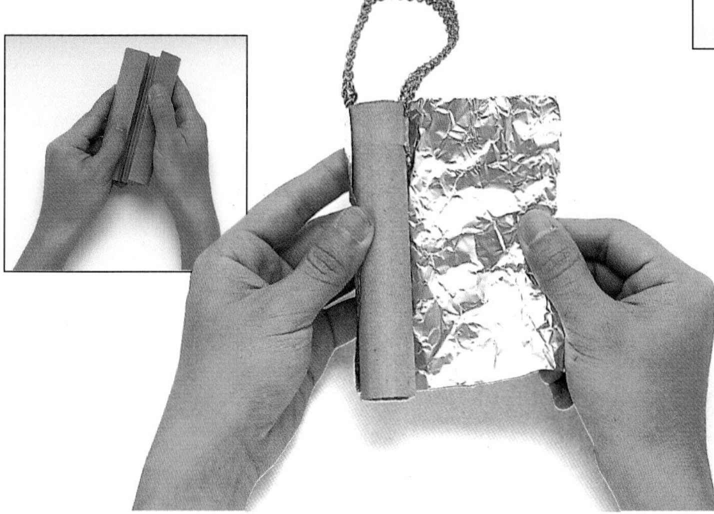

3 Roll the cardboard to make a handle. Attach the braid to make a carrying strap. Cover the handle with aluminum foil. Use the colored tapes to hold it in place and decorate the handle.

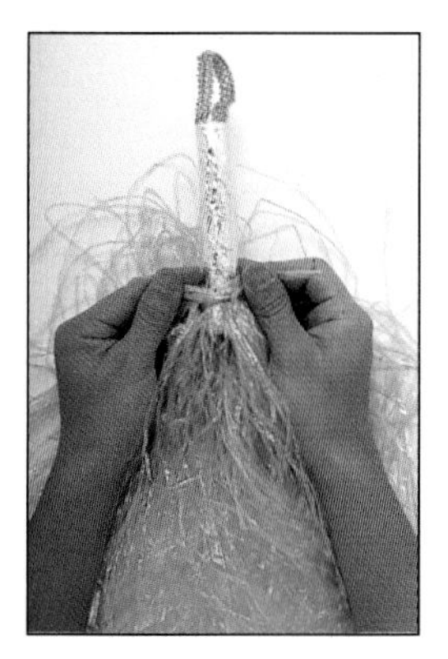

4 Push the end of the handle into the raffia tail so that the tail hides the end of the handle and stays firmly in place. Add fringe around the bottom of the handle.

Make Rice Pancakes

The Arabs brought rice and spices to Kenya when they arrived on the coast centuries ago. Their influence can be tasted in the food of the Swahilis living on the coast. These spicy pancakes would be a nice treat for Maulidi.

You will need:

1. 1 teaspoon active dry yeast
2. $\frac{1}{2}$–1 cup (120–240 ml) warm water
3. 1 cup (200 g) sugar
4. $2\frac{3}{4}$ cups (385 g) rice flour
5. $\frac{1}{4}$ teaspoon ground cardamom
6. $\frac{1}{4}$ cup (60 ml) canned coconut milk
7. $\frac{1}{2}$ cup (120 ml) vegetable oil
8. A large bowl
9. A frying pan
10. Measuring cups
11. A spatula
12. A wooden spoon
13. Measuring spoons
14. A dish towel (not terrycloth)

1 Dissolve the yeast in 1/2 cup (120 ml) warm water. Add a pinch of sugar and set aside in a warm place for 5 minutes. The mixture should foam up.

2 In the bowl, combine sugar, flour, and cardamom. Add the coconut milk and the yeast mixture and stir. It should be like pancake batter. If it's too thick, add a little water until it runs slowly from the spoon.

3 Cover the bowl with a towel and set aside in a warm place for about 1 hour or until the mixture has nearly doubled in size.

4 Heat 1 tablespoon oil over medium-high heat. Pour 1/2 cup (120 ml) of batter into the pan and spread it to form a pancake. Cook until bubbles form, then turn over and cook the other side. Continue with the rest of the batter.

GLOSSARY

age set, 14	Group of people who were circumcised at the same time.
Bantu, 25	One of the four main groups of people in Africa.
boma, 12	A village.
chuka, 12	A cloak, usually red, that Maasai men wear for clothing.
circumcision, 12	Removal of parts of certain sexual organs in males and females.
clan, 16	A large group of people who are distantly related.
harambee, 8	Pull together.
lunar, 6	Following the phases of the moon.
moran, 15	Maasai warrior.
Mzee, 11	Swahili word meaning "Old One" or "Wise One."
Ngai, 15	Name given to Supreme Creator by Maasai and Kikuyu.
olaiguenani, 12	Age set leader appointed at initiation.
olotuno, 19	Age set leader appointed at Eunoto.
Swahili, 8	Language widely spoken in East Africa.

INDEX

Picture credits
Camerapix: 7 (bottom),10 (bottom),25 (both); David Keith Jones/ Images of Africa: 2, 3 (bottom), 5, 8, 9 (top), 14, 17, 18, 19 (bottom), 22 (top), 23, 28; Christine Osborne: 3 (top), 24; Carla Signorini Jones/ Images of Africa: 4, 6 (left); Susanna Burton: 6 (right), 11; Still Pictures: 7 (top), 10 (top), 12, 13 (both), 15 (bottom), 19 (top), 20, 21 (bottom); Hulton Deutsch: 9 (bottom); Hutchison Library: 15 (top), 16 (top), 22 (bottom); Image Bank: 21 (top); Liba Taylor: 16 (bottom), Hoaqui: 1.